Nephi Gets the Brass Plates

written by Tiffany Thomas
illustrated by Nikki Casassa

CFI · An imprint of Cedar Fort, Inc · Springville, Utah

HARD WORDS:
brother, brass, plate

PARENT TIP: Have the child use a finger, craft stick, twig, or other item to point to each word as they read.

This is Nephi.

Nephi is a
man of God.

These are Nephi's brothers.

God tells them
to get the
brass plates.

This is Laban.

Laban has the brass plates.

Laban is
very bad.

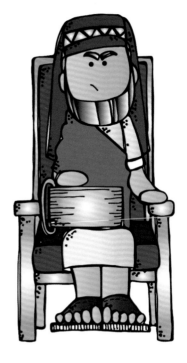

Nephi does not get
the brass plates.

9

Nephi's brothers are mad.

Nephi gets
the brass plates.

Nephi's brothers are not mad.

The end.

ISBN 13: 978-1-4621-4337-5

Published by CFI, an imprint of Cedar Fort, Inc. • 2373 W. 700 S., Suite 100, Springville, UT 84663
Distributed by Cedar Fort, Inc., www.cedarfort.com

Cover design and interior layout design by Shawnda T. Craig
Cover design © 2022 Cedar Fort, Inc.
Printed in China • Printed on acid-free paper
10 9 8 7 6 5 4 3 2 1